Art Therapy Workbook for Grief & Loss:

Exploring the experience of grief through art therapy & writing exercises.

By Emily Bell M.A., LPCC, Art Therapist

For Tony

"I carry your heart with me, I carry it in my heart."

E.E. Cummings

Welcome

Starting an art therapy practice can be a powerful tool in your
self care routine. If you are new to the practice of art therapy, it's definition
is simple: engaging in creativity for emotional wellbeing.
Many people find art therapy to be a powerful agent for
change because of it's mind- body connection; accessing parts of us that words
alone cannot express.

The art therapy exercises in this workbook are inspired and adapted from
ideas of therapists, healers, meditation instructors, poets, artists, Zen Buddhists,
my personal journey with grief, and most importantly; folks
I've been lucky enough to support through my work as an art therapist.

Any/all art media are welcome, although you don't need any materials besides
a drawing/writing utensil and this journal to get started. Suggestions for art
materials are only suggestions. These exercises are written in terms
of drawing and writing; however, painting, collage, modeling with clay, or any
other art material is welcome. Everyone has an inner artist;
let your creativity fly without judgement. No prior art experience is needed.

The goal of this workbook is for personal expression and not for art critique.
If you notice criticisms of your art starting to creep into your
journaling practice, gently remind yourself: your art is valid and
worthy just as it is right now, without needing any technical skill or training.
The therapeutic benefits of art can be found in the process of creating it,
just as much in the finished product.

Create space for yourself to enjoy the creative process.

A note on Grief & Loss

Grief is a word that describes a variety of emotions, sensations, thoughts or behaviors that people may experience following a loss. Grief is normal, even animals grieve! However, grief can be challenging to process. There's no right or wrong way to grieve; we all do it differently.

Elizabeth Kubler-Ross was a psychiatrist and author who laid the foundation of how we conceptualize these experiences. Kubler-Ross outlined stages in grief and loss. The stages include denial, depression, bargaining, anger, acceptance. However you may experience many of these stages simultaneously, with nuances & a wide depth of different emotions, or skip stages; no one's experience of grief is the same.

No matter what your experience with grief is, remember you aren't alone. There are national resources at the end of this workbook.

How to use this workbook

All prompts can be done realistically, abstractly represented or anywhere in between; artistic license is welcome.

Suggestions for art materials are only suggestions. Use the art materials that you have access to, you don't need to purchase new art media to benefit from this workbook.

Keep this workbook somewhere private, treat it like a diary.

The prompts in this journal start with mindful art therapy exercises and progressively increase in depth. If you feel overwhelmed at any time, return to the beginning mindfulness prompts.

Making art and grieving are similar in that there's no right or wrong way to do it, I invite you to practice leaving any judgments or expectations to the side. In Art Therapy, what makes your art "good", is that you made it, and you are worthy just as you are right now without doing or changing anything.

Suggested Supply List

Markers
Watercolor Paints
Colored Pencils
Pens
Collage material (old magazines,
patterned paper, colored paper, etc.)
Glue stick
Oil Pastel
Drawing Pencils

**Any/all art media are welcome, although you don't
need any materials besides a drawing/ writing
utensil and this journal to get started. Suggestions
for art materials are only suggestions.

This workbook belongs to:

Who or What I've lost:

How my life has changed:

Practicing mindfulness (bringing our awareness to the present moment), is a useful tool when navigating grief.

A simple way to practice mindfulness is to use our breath If you feel overwhelmed, turn your attention to your breath. A deep breath signals to our bodies that we are safe.

Grieving is a process that takes a tremendous amount of physical, emotional, and mental energy. Therefore, deserves self-compassion above all else. Take care, find a safe place, rest, drink water, breathe, and express.

Fill the following pages with circles, triangles, and squares; big and small. Try to fill the entire page, leaving no open space.

Suggested materials: pens, pencils, markers
Date:

WRITING REFLECTION:

What title would you give your drawing and why? Do the shapes or colors represent anything to you? Do they remind you of anything?

Date:

Pick some objects within view around you, without picking up your pencil or looking at the paper, draw the objects.

Suggested materials- pen or pencil

Date:

RELFECTION QUESTIONS:

Describe your drawings. How would you title the picture?

Date:

Turn your focus inward; notice your breathing. Is it short, smooth, quick? Use lines to draw your breath.

Art Materials: Pencils, Pens, or markers

Date:

Describe your breath, did it change as you started to focus on it? What do you notice about the lines you drew?

Date:

Using your non-dominant hand, fill following pages with lines, scribbles, and colors.

Suggested Materials: Colored Pencil, Markers, Pens, Drawing Pencils.
Date:

Reflect on the experience of using your non-dominant hand, was it hard to let go of control? Did you feel silly, uncomfortable? What words come to mind as you look over the last few pages?

Date:

Using both hands at the same time, fill the pages with lines, as if there was a mirror down the middle of the paper.

Re: Pen, Pencil, Marker

Date:

WRITING REFLECTION QUESTIONS:

What did you notice within yourself, while working on the mirror image line drawings? How did you feel about the process? What thoughts and emotions came up for you?

Date:

Grief is an experience filled with a variety of emotions, sensations, and experiences. Sometimes grieving means experiencing many emotions simultaneously, at times those emotions can conflict with one another.

There is no one way to process grief. No two people experience it the same. Navigating through the grief process is complex, it takes time, practice, & self compassion.

Emotions of Grief Wheel

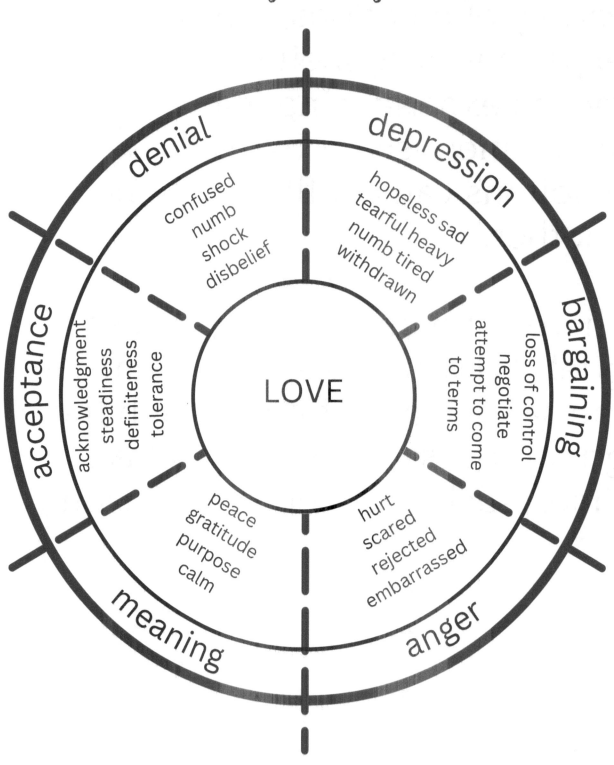

The Grief Emotion Wheel is a small example of what some people may experience as a result of a loss.

Use this space to include emotions, sensations or behaviors you have noticed, that weren't included on the emotion wheel. They can be in any order.

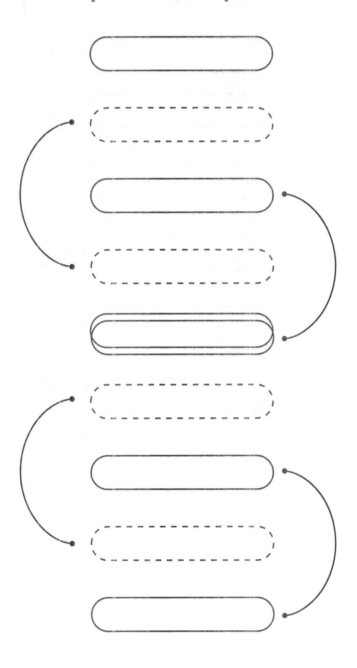

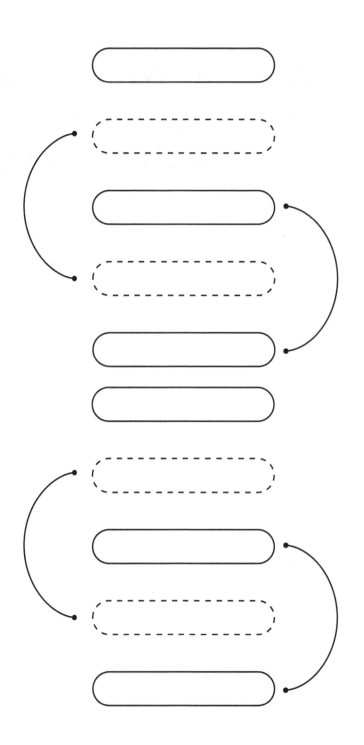

Assign colors to each emotion you have experienced.

Re: oil pastel, paint, markers, colored pencils

Date:

color   emotion/ sensation/behavior

◯ _____

◯ _____

◯ _____

◯ _____

◯ _____

◯ _____

◯ _____

◯ _____

◯ _____

◯ _____

◯ _____

◯ _____

color   emotion/ sensation/behavior

◯ _____

◯ _____

◯ _____

◯ _____

◯ _____

◯ _____

◯ _____

◯ _____

◯ _____

◯ _____

◯ _____

◯ _____

Layer all the colors that represent your grief process

Colored pencils, markers, paint, oil pastels

Date:

Reflect on the variety & layers of complex emotions.

Date:

ART THERAPY PROMPT:

Grieving is hard work, it's important to give yourself time to rest. Create an image that represents a safe place to rest, or the feeling of being held and secure. This could be a nest, cave, chrysalis, a place in nature; somewhere real or imaginary.

Colored pencils, oil pastels, paint, collage
Date:

What do you need to feel secure, rest, and take a break. Are there people, things, or places that provide extra support or comfort? Describe what your safe place feels, looks, smells, and sounds like.

Date:

Many people experience grief like waves of an ocean, moving up and down, coming in and out like the tide.

Anniversaries, birthdays, holidays, the time of year of the loss, or other special events are times you may experience big waves of grief. I refer to these as tidal waves, because you may be able to predict its timing.

Some days may appear to have calm waters, and clear skies; yet we find ourselves struck by a rogue wave of grief. Unpredictable by nature, we can find ourselves overwhelmed unexpectedly by grief experiences.

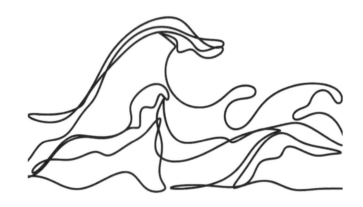

Grief is often felt in waves; coming in and out like the ocean tides. Create an image of what a wave of grief has felt like for you.

Oil pastel, paint, colored pencil, collage
Date:

WRITING REFELCTION:

Recall a time you've experienced a wave of grief, what do you notice? What are your thoughts, feelings, or actions like? How long did it last? Did anything help while you waited for it to pass?

Date:

Write a letter to your loss. Are there things you've been wanting to say, release, or get off your chest? After writing it out; imagine a wave taking out to sea anything you're ready to let go.

Date:

Active ocean volcanoes can be a good metaphor for any anger you may notice related to grief.

Consider a time you may have felt anger related to grief & create an image of anger as a volcanic eruption giving shape to the feeling. This can be realistic, abstract or anywhere in between.

Hand torn collage, oil pastel, marker, paint
Date:

Describe your image in detail. What do the colors and shapes represent to you? What would you title this image? Are there outside triggers that spark anger for you?

Date:

Outlets for Anger

Volcanoes and anger have something in common. Both can be big, powerful, or even scary at times.

When undirected & uncontained, volcanoes and anger can cause destruction. On the other hand, both can be a powerful agent of change. Ocean volcanoes, when the flow is directed, can create new land and islands.

Over time, waves from the ocean, cool and smooth out lava. Just like over time the waves of grief we experience will soothe big emotions. As waves cool lava a black shiny rock called obsidian is created. Obsidian is lightweight, and can be a useful tool and reminder.

As you navigate the waves of grief, you are calming and shaping your experience that, in time, will feel lighter, easier to walk around with.

Because of the light weight of obsidian, it is something we can carry with us without feeling heavy or weighed down; just like the love we have for what or who we lost.

Create an image of a favorite memory, or nostalgic emotion, related to your loss.

paint, colored pencil. marker
Date:

Write about your memory. What is your favorite part? What do you want to carry with you about this memory?

Date:

Use lines, shapes, and colors to create an image of love.

Oil pastels, paint, marker, colored pencil
Date:

Write a story about love & your loss.

Date:

Remember, the love you feel for who or what you lost can be with you, whenever you need. Like a piece of light-weight obsidian in your pocket.

Simply, close your eyes and recall some of your favorite memories & emotions to your mind.

Create an image of some time in the future. What elements do you hope to see there? What do you need there?

Collage materials

Date:

Describe the image of the future you created. What are some of your favorite parts about it? What feels important to include? Are there places to create, purpose or meaning?

Date:

Honoring your loss & Moving forward.

Some people consider life after a loss like a new normal. Creating new traditions or customs within a new normal can keep us connect to what we lost in a new way. Remembering your loss honors your grief journey and loved one.

EXAMPLES OF TRADITIONS TO REMEMBER LOSS

Cooking a favorite meal
lighting a candle in memory
do a favorite activity
listen to your loved ones favorite songs
dance, sing
write a song about them
paint a favorite memory
tell stories of your loved one
remember funny memories you shared
look at pictures
perform a random act of kindness in their honor
Create a garden in their honor
Make/write them a card
Spend time with loved ones

What would new traditions will you try?

_____

_____

_____

_____

_____

You've made it to the end of this workbook.

What will you take with you from this experience? What have you learned about yourself or grief?

Remember, grief is a natural and normal experience found across the natural world. There's no wrong way to grieve, no two people will grieve the same way.

You've honored yourself and your loss by taking time to slow down and process your experience.

Resources

www.counseling.org

healgrief.org

good-grief.org

griefcounselor.org

nacg.org

griefshare.org

ekrfoundation.org

Thank you
other works by this author:

www.amazon.com/author/openmindtherapy

Mandala a day: Art Therapy Journal

Shared Family Art Therapy Journal

Art Therapy Journal for Adults &
Teens

Art Therapy Journal for
LGBTQIA+ youth

OPEN MIND
therapy

Emily Bell is a licensed professional clinical counselor, art therapist,
and owner of Open Mind Therapy LLC.
She lives in works in the Twin Cities
and aspires to increase access to support for emotional wellness.
She has worked with people
of all ages and believes everyone
has an inner artist that deserves to express themselves.

Made in United States
Troutdale, OR
11/27/2023

14953101R00060